My Daughter
LISTEN TO
YOUR FATHER

Be cautious   Be careful   Be safe

Live Happily

A survival guide for every young woman's purse

Mark Spurling

First printing: 2017

ISBN-13: 978-0998783314

mlspurlingauthor@gmail.com

U.S. Trade bookstores and wholesalers please reach out via email

My Daughter
LISTEN TO
YOUR FATHER

This is not just a book; but the truth revealed to all daughters about men, relationships, careers, and so much more. This book is based on a young women's questions, concerns and personal thoughts shared with her father and his guidance to help assure her that she would be prepared for life and all to come.

And he said to her gently...

My daughter, just listen...

Preface

I'm writing to you because I love you and I want you to succeed in your life. I want you to be as beautiful as you are and as smart as you want to be. I want you to dream and know that all of your dreams can come true. Spread your wings my daughter and fly. Soar as high as you want to and go as far as you want to go. Be a scientist, a beautician or a CEO. Travel the world. Make friends and fall in love. It's your life and it's your world.

I'm not writing this to tell you what to do. This is not to shelter you. But I'm merely trying to set up some guidelines for the basis of a good foundation. First and foremost, know that learning continues long after high school and that life is full of lessons to be learned.

Always remember that I love you and I'm proud of you. And no matter what you do I'm honored to be you father.

On February 21, 2014 I received a phone call and my oldest daughter, a teenager in high school, being wild and boy crazy, came to live with me. She was out of control and I was unprepared and I didn't know what to expect;

but I knew in that very moment I could not let her down.

Raised by her mother and step dad she did great in school.She was kind, respectful and sweet; but I knew it was my job to mold and prepare her for the situations that could possibly cause her to stumble, fall and get off to a poor start in life. Struggling and living in lack was nothing I wanted for any of my daughters. I want them to flourish and be able to fly.

The opening paragraphs above came from the letter I started writing to my daughter that gave birth to this book and I believe it could be the start of a new beginning and a new mission for our daughters to come.

This could be the movement that would help change their lives.

Dedication

My Daughters

I dedicate this book to my daughters whom I made the promise to always be there to encourage them, love them, protect them and participate actively in their lives.

My Dad

To my dad who always encouraged me to write when I was younger and inspired me to dream big.

Welcome to Adulthood

My daughter by now you've graduated high school; and hopefully, on your way to college. Know that now it's time to truly start your life. The future is today. And yesterday is the past. Know that there's plenty of things involved in" living your life"; but always remember to live happily, be healthy and safe.

I strongly recommend developing a plan or goals for yourself right from the beginning. Your life is like a movie. You're the director, writer, costume designer and the star. There are others characters; but remember you're the star in your life. Other people will come along and try to occupy the main role. But it's yours to hold on to or give away. I strongly recommend holding on to it. In other words don't let someone else move into your life and take it over.

I remember when I was a teenager there were boys and girls I grew up with and some I went to school with. Most we're cool, dressed in style, stayed with the latest trends and pretty much had freedom to do mostly what they wanted.

I remember one day playing basketball in our yard with a group of about 7-10 boys. My dad came home from work and immediately asked probably 6 or 7 boys to get out of the yard. I got upset and embarrassed at the time; but I was young and didn't understand. Later in life I realized my dad was only protecting me. Those boys either went to jail, got caught up in drugs, or something worse.

As the group of boys and girls I grew up with got older most of us hung out at clubs, experienced drinking, stayed out late at night, started having sexual encounters and got into trouble a little bit here and there. But as the years went by some of us broke out into different directions and started making our own ways in life. Some moved out on their own, joined the military, or parents got them good jobs. Quite a few went to college. Some graduated some didn't. A few landed pretty decent jobs working for the state, city, or the federal government and that could be pretty good. A few went into the medical field, education, and private sector jobs. This group did very good as well. Now, a very small hand full went into business for themselves, real estate and sales & marketing.

This group does extremely well. But now back to the majority.

Most today are still were they were ten, and even twenty years ago. Hanging out, partying, and doing what they do most which is probably nothing at all. Some of the people in this category got caught up having babies to early and got stuck in this part of life because being young and taking care of kids is very difficult and nearly impossible to do effectively without help and financial stability.

They struggle, day care is to expensive and you can't really trust the neighbor anymore. So when you do the numbers, this person usually ends up on government assistance for the next 18- 20 years. Others never fully matured mentally pass the early stages and they're possibly just stuck in a life cycle. For example, my grandmother, grandfather, mom, dad and now me we're all stuck in this rut riding the bus, driving an old beat up car and struggling barely getting by month in and month out. They're thinking and wishing life for them and their three kids were different.

Getting the picture yet? Avoid the traps of young life as often as possible. Babies, becoming an addict, alcoholic, prostitution, ruining your credit because you don't know it's value, theft or doing something even dumber which lands you in prison like murder.

Young adults ruin their lives almost daily at this age and the judicial system is all to quick to lock them up and do what? That's right! Throw away the key.

All I'm saying is at this point in your life you should be saying to yourself that you want more. I eventually want a career and a good paying job, a house, a new car, vacationing, money in the bank, or a really good opportunity. Start positioning for these things by mentally conditioning yourself to break out from the pack of the majority and start making your own way.

I heard once that the majority of the worlds' wealth is held by a very small handful of the worlds' population. Also that most people rarely reach their dreams and less than a third of the people have no distinctive dreams or goals for themselves at all.

When I was a kid I heard my granddad say to my dad, "Son if I was a young man. I would ..." and about 25 years later I heard my dad say the same thing to me. My dad spent most of my life trying to protect me, help me, guide me and encourage me to be good, better, and then the best I can be. He helped me understand that I am a work in progress and it's up to me to pave my way. Along the way I'll get a little help here and there but ultimately it is up to me.

At this stage in my life I now realize my dad is my friend, my teacher and my HERO. But I'm going share with you a lot of things he never shared with me.

Table of Contents

Is it Time to go to Work

You've graduated high school and it may seem like it's time to rest and relax. You're probably thinking maybe you could take a couple of years off. Nope, this shouldn't happen. You should be on your way to college somewhere; but if you're not, maybe it's time to go to work.

I urge you to develop a plan and quick if you don't already have one. Winging it, is not an option because in five or ten years you'll still be winging it, feeling trapped and stuck in that rut trying to figure out a game plan and wishing you went to college or trade school somewhere. By then my daughter you'll be close to thirty something. Working a dead end job, on a train going absolutely nowhere is not where you want to be. There's no light at the end of this tunnel. Go to college. Get it out of the way.

Becoming a security guard, cashier or any other type of job that fit into this category long term and earning nine dollars an hour is a sure way to tell that you're not on track, nor are you in control.

If you're making ten dollars per hour or less and feeling like you're losing your mind you should take a hard look at yourself and plan on continuing your education.

At minimum wage or near it you need two full time jobs just to pay the bills and enjoy a little entertainment every now and again. And that's eighty hours a week! Guess what my daughter! You are now tired as all get out.

Not to mention, if by chance, you do go this route, you could end up being stuck with a buster for a boyfriend weighing you down like an anchor and convincing you daily that you can't do better. His biography consist of felonies like assault, drug charges, burglary and a gun charge which has caused him to go in and out of jail over the years. And by the time you are lucky enough to get him he can't work a job.

Watch out, you better call 911! Because pretty eyes, with the good hair and six pack abs, just got angry and grabbed you by your neck. You better be careful.

So, forget about a boyfriend that could possibly be "The One"; or consistently hanging out having fun with your girlfriends because there's no real chanceof having a positive relationship or any type of life because you're to busy. Money wise, you're doing ok for just starting out; but try keeping it up for a few years. It gets old really quick. This is no way to continue. My daughter it's to hard. And it's a quick burnout. If you're doing it with a purpose, to buy a car, furnish your new place, pay off some debt and it's temporary, by all means go for it.

If you're actually deciding to go to work full time know and accept what it really means to do so. The key and purpose is to support yourself. If you're not continuing your education you'll be figuring out how to manage solely on your own. By the end of the first year there will probably be no more handouts from the adults in your life. No more shopping sprees, trips to the salon, no more pocket money. You'll start to be weaned off gradually and then eventually cold turkey. Snip, snip at this point, you will start feeling like you're on your own. But you're not. The goal here is to transition you into adulthood by giving you a little bit of responsibility to go along with that new found freedom of being totally out of school and having you own money. What? Did you think you were just going to be able to blow your cash on nothing but you.

Work is basically what you will do for income to take care of yourself financially. It can be physical labor as in the jobs where you see people driving a route getting in and out of a truck delivering packages or something like that, to construction. Yeah, I've seen women construction workers out there on the job with hard hats on working and getting all sweaty. It can be mental like managing people and procedures. It could very well be phones all day, sitting in front of a computer screen, pushing paper work or cleaning up and caring for people in their old age.

Just starting out your new job could be a wide array of just about anything. Needless to say it's going to be what you choose or fall into.

Be smart about it. Right out of high school I fell into the bank teller job and earned five dollars per hour. And nearly ten years later I chose real estate working for a top homebuilder in that period where I was earning over one hundred thousand dollars per year.

My daughter with the internet you literally have the world at your fingertips. Take your time, look around, explore and figure out the direction you want your work to go into and take that journey. You might not start out where you want to be; you may even get comfortable and then knocked down a few times; but understand day by day and as the years move forward you'll move toward your goals. It's a process. And eventually you'll settle into a job out there that will work for you. Just don't settle into a low paying one that will keep you struggling and trying to live on payday loans or in and out of pawnshops. But if you fall in love and marry a rich guy; by all means, take up a cause and do volunteer work.

Know that jobs pay according to titles and duties. For example a clerk, at a grocery store, at an auto dealership; or working for the city may require similar skill sets but will pay totally different. And a sales associates' pay will vary from industry to industry. My titles working over the years were either sales associate, sales counselor, sales representative, or sales executive and the duties and experience rarely changed but the income did, and drastically. Little things like this make the biggest difference between four or five dollars per hour and sometimes much more.

So if you wake up one morning moving a little slower than you use to, and you're no longer in that single digit size pair of jeans you're probably really close to that ten year mark. And if you're still just getting by you better do a double take because it's really time to do something different. I have friends that went back to school and changed careers in their forties.

Over the years I've met people with various back grounds. Their levels of education were different. And their outlook and mindset on life were extraordinarily different as well. Know that experiences and exposures in life influence the way we think and what we do and what we believe. Life afforded different opportunities for some and misfortune for others.

I've met professional men and women who have started climbing the corporate ladders in their industries and live in big lavish lifestyles at the top of their careers because of hard work, dedication and the guts to dream big and chase their dreams. And this is normal to them.

And I've also had the privilege of meeting people that struggle day in and day out trying to figure out everything, on their own, as they go. They struggle to pay the rent, lights and take care of their children. I've seen people go to work faithfully to get a paycheck that was not enough. And next year it still won't be enough. They'll probably struggle their entire lives. Growing up their families struggled, their friends struggled and now they struggle because that's all they know. Ultimately, how well you do in life or not, boils down to your surroundings and the decisions you make.

Quite a few of the professional men and women I've met have high paying jobs where they meet to discuss other meetings and manage the people in charge who hire and manage the other people in charge. These people are in upper level management and director positions and these career level jobs require education and letters behind their names.

My daughter if this is your dream; know that you have to study, work hard and pay your dues. Put your mind to it because you can accomplish whatever you set out to do. But if it's not, it's ok because this is not the only way.

In this chapter I just want you to know that you need to, and you should go to school. Make plans to educate yourself because some type of education or certification is better than none and it gives you an advantage when it comes to career choices and making money. And never settle for a man that's going to drag you down.

Know that in life it's not all about money and money is not everything. There are other things just as important like family, time, education and good health. But, money will get you very close to where you want to be. And it will definitely put a smile on your face most days especially when you're traveling across the ocean on a cruise ship; or in another country spending time with family, good friends and in good health.

My daughter, I'd rather see you struggling to choose which outfit and pair of shoes to wear. You're frustrated because you're not sure which floor plan or neighborhood to move into. Torn between which new job offer you should accept and sad because one of your good friends couldn't get off work to make the trip. Versus being frustrated, torn, and sad because you don't have enough money to fix your car, lights off, rent due and you're constantly struggling to make ends meet.

I want you to have everything you dream of; and again know that all of your dreams can come true. **Work can be fun, exciting and fulfilling. Or it can be mundane, stressful, and exhausting. Either way know that you got to go to work and it should pay well.**

College Degrees
Certifications & licenses

If you decide to go to college you have to always remember why you are there. Set your goals, write them down, post on the wall, and focus, focus, and focus.

College is a place where the people that are there are from all over the world in most cases. It is very diverse in culture and easy to get distracted. So study hard, play just a little and make very smart friends.

Understand that people go to college for several different reasons for example to meet new people and make connections. Some go because it sounds like a good idea at the time. Others go to party and join fraternities or sororities. Most go for all of the above; but ultimately it's about that piece of sheep skin to hang on the wall. A degree will make the biggest difference in your life my daughter make sure you get one. Then go back and get another when you find the need.

I believe people that go to college and make good grades, pledge and make friends have the most fun in college and have the greatest potential to get off to a great start very early on in life. It's ok to make time to party and have a little fun along the way but remember why you're there.

A degree will help unlock and open doors that would never open ordinarily on their own. Most of the highest paying job titles and careers are tied to college degrees. Make no mistake without it life's journey will be rough and you'll work extremely hard just to be a little below average. But it is possible.

Going to college by no means is it going to be easy. That's why you need smart friends determined to graduate. But If by chance you find that a university and a "four year degree" is not for you know that I'll still love you. Because in reality I know college is not for everyone. If it's not for you a contingency plan is definitely a must.

Community college is a good alternative because with the right training, certifications and license you can be off to a great career in a booming industry specifically related to that training. Some industries pay very well and you could be working in just a couple of years or less.

Just know that a four year degree and or specialized training will certainly give you an advantage and a leg up in life. So do some research and figure out what you would like to do and definitely find out which careers pay the big bucks.

Please know and understand that as an adult you will have responsibilities and in most cases those responsibilities usually equate to paying your bills. Not making enough money will cause you to have to struggle, go without necessities and do things for money you really don't want to do.

I've met people who complicated their whole lives when they were young because they struggled financially and made bad choices and ended up with jail time and records that will follow them their entire lives. And this is no joke my daughter if it don't belong to you don't steal it.

And luxuries, forget about them because you'll be busy just trying to keep a roof over your head, food in your belly and the lights on. Make the decision to get more education after high school. You're going to need it.

Dead end Jobs
Versus Good Jobs & Careers

My daughter being young is a gift in itself. Treasure your energy and learn to value your time because your time is precious. Protect your time and energy because right now it's on your side and will be for the next fifteen years or so. There is very little you can't accomplish with focus, direction, and just a little bit of that energy. You've got plenty of time to play and have fun; but let's get serious for just a moment. When it comes to choosing a job, I'm just going to tell you like it is. Some jobs I would prefer you don't waste your time with. Others will be what you make of it. Ideal job opportunities will stand out most. Keep your eyes and ears open and don't be so quick to settle.

When you hear words like seasonal, temporary, part time, high turnover and minimum wage proceed forward with caution or perhaps go the other way all together. These type jobs will usually get you nowhere and leave you frustrated. So truthfully, don't bother unless you find yourself without options or just really needing a second job. If you only need it for what it's truly worth you're doing great. Needing extra money for the holidays or to treat yourself to something nice that's not normally in the budget then seasonal and temporary sounds ideal. But again, if you're needing it long term you should definitely reevaluate your work situation.

I've met several guys and women over the years that started out on fries and worked their way up to store, district and regional management positions. If you have drive, ambition and a winning personality you can too. But if not, then classify this as a dead end job. If you're not moving up then clock out. There is no need of being thirty and still frying chicken and fries or selling tickets at a movie theater for minimum wage.

Figure out the differences when choosing a job by looking at the people that already work there. If half the workers are complaining, trying to figure out how to escape; or they're always broke and skipping lunch this is a sure sign as well. My daughter be cautious. I started a temporary job and ended up being stuck there for nearly three years and I hated every minute of it. I made the most of it; but I don't wish this for you.

Now on the other hand, know that when you find a good job things will be totally different. Employees have nice new cars in the parking lot or garage. You hear people saying things like, this is the only job I've ever had. You know Mr. Jones is retiring after 35 years. Girl I'm going on vacation next month. Don't forget to look over your benefits package. Stocks, bonds, insurance and 401k are all buzz words that should have you thinking long term. This job can come from any fortune 100 or 500 company ideally and various government jobs to most major companies. These type jobs offer opportunities in different departments, other cities and foreign countries. A chance to move up, make more money and go to school if need be are all part of the deal.

Also know that these companies provide excellent career opportunities as well for people who decided to go to school and specialize in fields like accounting, business management, public relations and other long term endeavors when people figure out what they love.

Uh oh! I'm getting excited for you. This could be an opportunity of a life time. And guess what? You might even find a husband there. I said might. You'll probably run into that player and that down low guy as well. So be prepared to handle your business and protect yourself.

Here's a little nugget for your purse. Whenever I was out and about and saw people dressed nicely, or in nice cars looking like they had good jobs or careers I would always ask what type of work they were in. I was curious to know if they went to college, and sometimes, if where they were working was hiring. This always kept me informed. In most cases I usually made similar money or they had a certificate or degree that disqualified me. And that always hurt. Again, my daughter with the internet you don't have to guess or settle. Figure it out and make it happen.

There are plenty of good jobs and just as many dead end jobs out there so do your research, sharpen your interviewing skills, get your best business outfit ready and choose wisely. **And if by chance you chose wrong know that you're never stuck. Get back out there and interview again.**

My daughter the world is your pocketbook, spend, spend, spend wheel and deal. If you've got that old entrepreneurial spirit and you're dreaming of going into business for yourself go for it. Listen to your heart and follow your dreams. I've heard people say do what you love and you'll never work a day in your life.

Business can be tuff and very rewarding. It's got ups and downs; but in the end I promise if you work smart, do it right, and stay focused it will be worth it. No matter what you do it can be a huge success. There is nothing better than working for yourself.

Keep in mind nothing worth having comes easy. And in most cases people fail several times before they succeed. Above all think big. You might start out small but the skies the limit. **Who knows, your idea for a home based business or corner shop could end up being global and people could know your name and product lines around the world.**

Why I chose Sales, Marketing & Real estate

My daughter, know that when I started out young in life, things were the same for me as they are for you but they were very different. I sound like my dad with this statement. The more things change the more they remain the same. I've found this saying to be so true. I was young, unsure and kind of scared with my whole life in front of me.

I graduated high school, went to college, lost focus and didn't really have any priorities. I could say I spiraled out of control; but it would probably be better just saying I started out on the wrong track all together. But that's another story for later in itself.

I remember looking through the classifieds in the newspaper seeing job and career postings. Yeah, that's right. Back then we looked through the want ads in the newspapers for jobs. There was no internet yet. I use to dream of making thirty thousand dollars a year owning a house and starting a family. Oh and a car too! I didn't qualify to do much because I didn't really have any training or experience I was young without a clue. But that was my dream.

I realize now, back then, I didn't want much at all. I recall seeing a job posting for the airline. I don't remember the position posted but I did qualify for the position. I remember the job started out at five dollars an hour and there was a fifteen cents raise every year until top pay was reached which was about fifteen dollars an hour.

I remember doing the calculations in that moment to see what my income would be like and if that would get me closer to my dreams. I don't recall what the exact numbers were; but I did know those numbers didn't make sense to me at that time. It would have taken over twenty years to reach top pay. At this point in my life I imagine what it would've been like if I would have went down that path and I'm smiling.

When I looked at houses and cars in the newspaper along with jobs I knew one thing. It didn't add up. On paper there was no way to make it work. I mentioned before that I had friends that got good jobs because of their family members. I knew this was not a good job for me.

My mom was a home maker and my dad was self employed. I thought I didn't have any guidance boy was I wrong. But at this point in my life I had already slept through or ignored most of my dad's life lessons and I was going to do this on my own. But my eyes saw what my ears never heard.

I remember one Saturday after I had gotten fired from my banking job. By the way, this was the best thing that could have happened to me at this point. I was looking in the newspaper and I had a thought. What if I could get paid hourly plus earn extra money without working all the extra hours.

I needed two jobs in one. Then I saw the words hourly plus commission. Those words were like music to my ears and they changed my life. The idea of getting paid to talk and sell something sounded like a good idea to me at the time.

I would have never imagined that the core values my dad taught me while growing up would have shown up here. Honesty, integrity, ability to self motivate, time management and a willingness to succeed made me a great candidate to start out on a new path that would eventually become my career.

I started out working a job with a base pay plus comission then eventually just straight comission.

Since then my daughter every job for me has been based on performance and my uniform of choice became a shirt and tie and later in life a suit. My income and how much money I've gotten to take home over the years was solely based on me and I loved it. Over the years I've gotten big cash bonuses, vacations and awards. I could not imagine anything else.

Don't get me wrong it's been tough along the way and I've had my share of ups and downs; but my ups have been much higher and my downs were not as low. It was up to me if I succeeded or not. I made a choice to succeed.

To put things in perspective so you can actually understand. When it was tough I averaged twenty to twenty five dollars per hour. And when it was good I averaged close to fifty. I think I've done pretty good without long hard hours, burn outs, downsizing and layoffs. And without struggling to make ends meet.

Sales and marketing is an ideal opportunity for anyone wanting to live a lifestyle better than just regular and mundane. I've seen and met ordinary people generate extraordinary incomes that far exceed just paying the bills and there are plenty of people that fall into this category that make millions of dollars each year.

My daughter if I was a young man, sound familiar, I would have gotten a college degree because there are sales and marketing opportunities that pay even more than you can imagine. And there would be many more doors opened that I could walk through; instead they were closed to me. An education will not guarantee success; but it could carry you a great deal further in life long term.

The Difference between Friends and Associates

As you get older and start establishing yourself you'll need to know that different people come into your life for various different reasons. Some will show up to be a teacher. Some people will come along and teach some of life's simplest fundamentals. Be ready to listen and learn. Also be prepared to take notes and ask questions. Above all things understand what they're teaching.

Some will motivate and encourage you along your life's journey all the way to the end. Others will inspire you and shape you into whom you are to become. But also be aware because there are those who have a mission for some strange reason to tear you down, and they rarely have anything good to say about you. There are all types of people you will find in your circle. But none the less, know the difference.

I use to have a bunch of friends from all types of backgrounds. Or at least people that I thought were my friends until one day I realized the difference.

My dad and my mother's brother were close; and over the years if I was lucky, I could get them to talk. I realized that older people possessed wisdom and insight. My dad would tell me a story and then a year or two later my uncle would tell me the same exact story. Sometimes the length of time would span three or four years before I heard it from each; but none the less I always listened and took mental notes. Out of all the conversations I gathered I saw truly that my uncle and my dad were friends. My uncle didn't have any brothers; but He often told me if he could choose a brother he would choose my dad.

My uncle told me once before he passed away... "If you want a friend be a friend". I didn't think much of it at first but as I began to examine his words I started to understand that I am the key to me. In other words I realized I had the choice to pick and choose my friends. Who I opened up to and who I allowed to come into my circle. You have the same choice. Learn this early in your life.

I wouldn't dare try to pick your friends for you. I'll leave that up to you. But I will say this. It's ok if sometimes you have disagreements and fall out. It's ok if you stop talking for a while. If you don't spend as much time together as you use to that's ok too. Sometimes friends make you angry because they tell the truth or take the car keys because you had a little to much to drink. They'll tell you to your face that your man is no good because he's lazy or cheating. They come visit for the holidays if they can and show up at the hospital or when you least expect it. True friends are there until the very end and show up when you need them.

I learned to look at a person for who they truly are and if they have good intentions and a good heart. This type of person will be good, honest and fair in all their dealings with you and everyone else. This person nine time out of ten will not leave you in a jam, or pull you into one. And will help you stay out of trouble.

Associates are friends of friends and people you socialize with periodically depending on the weather. They often come and go. The associate can be a good asset to you or very detrimental. Be careful how you treat them and control your level of involvement. Some associates become friends and some friends end up as associates. But the reality is this; they didn't change who they are we just misread them.

I remember, when I was younger I had a friend. He was cool and we hung out together off and on over a couple of years. He was a really good friend I thought. Needless to say I ended up in situations where I was nearly jumped on and beat up. I had a gun pulled on me outside of a party one night and ended up getting involved with a lady who turned out to be living with, and taking care of, one of those pretty eyed, good hair, abs and bipolar type guys. He was weighing her down and she was searching for a way out. All because I was hanging out with my so called friend. I almost got caught up in the situation that got him killed too. But I heard a voice that said "no". And I've been listening to this voice ever since. I remember this as if it were yesterday.

Our lives were completely different and I know now that I should have kept him in the correct category of hi and by. Remember your good times may be different from someone else's.

Be friends with people who have similar interest and good moral fiber. You'll be able to trust them with your deepest secrets; or your life if you needed to. I didn't say tell your secrets though. But usually a small group of friends are all you need.

But know if you can't trust them deal with them accordingly. Sometimes it's just best to shut it down and walk away. Know that people have hidden agendas and even friends sometimes. Don't let broken friendships destroy you. Be cautious. After all, remember Judas and Brutus.

Some Girls Don't Make It Home

My daughter when you're young and in your twenties life's priority is almost just to party and have fun. But you need to be cautious. Know that some girls leave home and don't make it back.

People offer rides and there's someone you don't really know already in the car or they pick them up after you. The person(s) in the car could be a class mate, coworker, neighbor or just someone you see quite often, periodically or a total stranger.

I've heard dozens of stories where young women willingly got into cars and ended up having to do something they didn't plan on doing in order to make it home that day. Girls have gotten abused, raped, beaten, and have come up missing all together.

I want you to think safety first when unsolicited or unexpected car rides pop up; or familiar situations suddenly take a twist. You need to be ready to say no thank you and ready to fight. No matter how far you have to walk or if your car is stalled on side of the road. If it's to hot or rainy, please don't take the chance. The risk is not worth it no matter what. This is what cellphones or Roadside services are for.

I've seen situations on the news and in my own part of town where girls have been picked up ten minutes from home and ended up thirty miles across the city. Some were lucky because they fought and managed to get away and get help after being lured and trapped.

Others were sexually assaulted by someone's friend, cousin, brother or an illicit uncle. Even worse, being found several days or weeks later naked and dead in the woods or buried in a field to sometimes never being found.

There are hundreds of stories like these that make the news across the country every year and probably thousands you never hear about from around the world. It could be the middle of the day, in the evening or a late night when someone or a group of people come along and offer you a ride. You never know.

I'm telling you this because I want you to be aware and alert and know in the blink of an eye situations can get way out of hand. And you need to know that the risk is high when hopping in cars. You have to be careful when getting in a car especially with a stranger or someone you don't totally trust.

KNOWING YOUR SELF WORTH

You grew up with your mother and I know she taught you plenty of very important things and I hope one of them was self-worth. I can't stress it enough. You have to know your self-worth. Seriously stop and figure this out. You have to know because if you don't people will under bid, under sell and undercut you. They will literally mow you down. And sell you for cheap. Literally!

Self-worth deals directly with your self-esteem. If you don't see the value in you nobody else will and it will be so easy for them to manipulate you into thinking less of yourself. **You are pretty, smart, intelligent, kind and you have a good heart. You are special and can do anything you put your mind to. Don't ever let anybody tell you otherwise.**

Understand, this can happen in every aspect of life; personal and professional. So call friends that want to use you; or cause you problems always with their hands out. Supervisors and coworkers that want to take advantage by forcing or pressuring you to help do their work; or demand you to pick up the slack. Friends have babies early in life and expect you to be responsible by babysitting and buying necessities. Sometimes you try to go along with it; but end up used and broke. They stop being your friend when you decide to stop letting them use you. These are just a few examples to get you thinking.

For now we'll talk about relationships. The average guy you meet is going to want one thing from you. It starts with an S and ends with X. That's right sex! Sex is the number one thing on a young man's mind clear into his thirties and talking about his conquest with his friends is the hottest topic. In my era guys had love letters, a bra, panties, and if he was lucky he had pictures to go along with his stories. But now days guys have technology. Cameras on phones, spy cams, video and internet all play a part in telling his dirty story. Someone's goodies just went viral last night with one million views. Lives get ruined and careers get destroyed every day. **Don't let it happened to you. Don't be and amateur video vixen for his pleasure only to be publicly humiliated online when you finally realize he's not the one. Or you decide to stop paying his bills and taking care of his children from his previous relationships.**

My daughter you are a rare pearl, a precious gem, a delicate flower. You have to respect yourself, love yourself, keep your panties up and know men are going to come and go. Not matter what the majority are not going to stay. Be smart and know your body is not for every man. Your time is not for just anybody. Your heart is not cheap. And your love is not for sale. Beware of men that show up baring gifts that are unwanted or unneeded. Children out of marriage, baby momma drama, I can't find a job because I don't work type men, come visit me in jail men, and let's stay together type men. All this mess will wear you down and keep you from getting focused and accomplishing you goals and reaching your dreams.

I'm not saying friends don't help friends. I'm not saying bosses are horrible and you shouldn't ever help your boyfriend. I'm saying I love you and I want you to be in a position to experience real happiness and prosperity in your life. Make sure relationships have value. "Don't let someone else pick a shade tree for you", as my father would.

And never forget this. There are men who become extremely good throughout their lives at breaking women down emotionally and psychologically as a form of control. You hear it oftentimes referred to as mental abuse. Words like fat, ugly and dumb should never be mistaken for words of love. Your pet name should never be demeaning. If he has to hurt your feelings to keep you in line you need to know you should not stay. If he's abusive verbally or physically he's not the one.

In my life I've seen women wrapped up in relationships that look like this and they've been convinced that this type of behavior is love and they live with black eyes, busted lips, and broken bones. My daughter this is not normal.

Being genuinely happy, healthy and safe are more important than this type of fictitious love. At all cost learn to love yourself first because this love cost to much and it's not worth it. Let me repeat myself again. My daughter it's not worth it. He is a loser and you will lose with him.

Everything you need to know About Boys and then some

Over my years of growing up I'd like to think I've become more mature and wiser. And looking back at situations that I've either been involved in, seen with my own eyes or heard first hand I'm going to tell you this about boys.

Boys are young men with great potential and awesome abilities that can catapult then into any arena in life they could possibly dream of. You're probably in high school with, or graduating college with the next NBA, NFL or MLB super star. The next Wall Street business man or Internet billionaire is probably the nerdy or unpopular kid that couldn't get your attention. I will tell you there are thousands of nobodies and sons of somebody who will grow up having a handle on life because they have parents who care. Mom and dad or grandparents will make sure their boys grow up to be descent and respectable men. These boys come in all shapes, sizes and colors. Some are short, tall, skinny, chubby, good looking, ugly, popular, and unpopular. Some have good hair, pretty eyes and six pack abs. They could be absolutely anybody. Make no mistake you will have to do a little homework to figure out who they are; but I'll get you started.

Quite a few cool and popular kids in school grow up in life not really living up to their full potential. And sometimes get into trouble before they graduate high school because their last few years in school are like a reality television show or a party. This rolls on in most cases for the next 2-4 years and even in college. But in most cases they're going to take a break after high school to socialize and hang out. The plan is to go to college after taking a break; but they live for the moment and find themselves later in life behind the eight ball usually still at home with mom or grandma and working a job they really don't want. At this point you will know exactly who they are because they are either in a borrowed car or on the bus dressed from head to toe with no plans of getting their own. Mom and grandma will take care of him financially and possibly ruining him right here allowing him to be irresponsible.

Ok, so here we go. Beware of boys with absentee fathers (Prison inmates) and no positive male figures in their live especially if they are being raised by the streets. Usually there's no job. They are out all night doing what they want without any real responsibilities and mom or grandma can't tell them what to do. His running buddies include guys home from jail. He will rob, steal, sell drugs and dress like the homies because he's affiliated with some sort of gang type click.

This particular boy is going to be misguided and stagnant in his life. He is going to lack decency and respect for himself and others which means he's is not going to know how to love and treat you. This boy is lost. And in most cases you are going to lose too if you have any dealings with him.

In most cases he's handsome with nice hair, pretty eyes and a nice smile. You have to ask him about his parents because it's likely he won't really know them or tell you about them. He's already part of a never ending cycle. Where is his dad?Probably in jail. Where is his mom? She's probably with her man. Thousands of young girls every year have sex and make babies with these guys. Not knowing these boys are on medication due to mental instabilities like bipolar disorder or schizophrenia or should be. Don't be a statistic.

This boy will make your life extremely difficult and he won't be anywhere around. He's not totally a bad guy, just lost. It's going to take him 10 years or so, jail time, getting shot, a murder case, or worse before he gets himself straight. Don't forget he's going to need those meds. By then he's got 3-4 kids and they're going to need medication too. This cycle never ends. I'm begging you to don't be part of it. And if he's going in and out the pokey chances are you don't want him no way.

Boys lie, steel, cheat, make babies, sell drugs, prostitute themselves, sleep with more than one woman at a time, have unprotected sex and sleep with other boys. Down low brothers have been around for years masquerading and portraying themselves as straight heterosexual men; but they're not. Beware of "Down Low" brothers.

Boys have HIV and other sexually transmitted diseases and they pass them along to girls. They rape, kill, abuse, use drugs, and tell you they love you in the midst of all of this. I'm not trying to scare you. Just pointing out that you need to keep your eyes open, guard up and make your own decisions. Be cautious, be careful be safe.

Just because he tells you he loves you or you're pretty doesn't give him the right to push you on your back and sleep with you unprotected. It doesn't give him the right to impregnate you and someone else at the same time. But he'll do it anyway because boys don't tell the truth and at this point don't really care.

You also need to know boys make babies and move on. But it takes two. Be responsible and protect yourself. I'm not boy bashing because your father was once a boy too. I'm just sharing with you things I've seen, heard, and know.

A boy can love you; but not be ready for you at that particular point in his life. He can have all the best intentions; but just will not do any of it right when it comes to you. You could even be the best possible girl for him and it still won't matter. At this point he's not ready nor is he going to commit to you or anybody else.

Pay attention and know when a boy is not going to commit. I've asked several ladies and neither could answer so I'll tell you so you'll know. Know that if he does not make it his business to communicate with you daily, add you into his plans for his future, does not introduce you to his parents or the people most important in his life. He's probably not going to commit to you. He'll do it eventually; but it won't be you. These are just guidelines to check by because some boys introduce everybody to their friends and family. Boys try and hold out and wait for the perfect someone; but usually that girl doesn't exist.

My daughter, I'm not hating on boys to try to persuade you in believing they're just horrible and no good. I want you to be prepared to set some standards and make ground rules. If you set the bar high enough and the boy really wants you he'll reach for you and step up and become a man.

Most young ladies ultimately dream of being married. You need to know your body is a sacred temple and you should treat it as such. Men want a woman they can treasure. Not a woman that's been misused, and abused physically or mentally with 3 or 4 kids. In everything you do treasure and love your body.

This type of guy will attract young ladies fresh out of high school. He's also the ideal catch for that college girl with a bright future, driving her parents insane because she's so in love. Not to mention, this guy sometimes gets early parole and makes it back in time for the corporate Christmas party or family reunion.

From your early twenties, thirties, forties and yes even fifties these men show up. And their criminal biographies are longer than my, ____ driving record. With all his baggage he will probably not be able to work. He might still be an anchor. You will take care of him. But if you're forty, stable and love him figure out.

Beware of The
"Down Low" Brother

You hear women everywhere saying this in their gossiping voice, "Girl not him look at him"! Girl he's tall, fit and sexy. He's got nice hair too. He's well groomed and don't forget about those eyes. Hum, yummy! Girl he's just your type of guy".

Or is he really? He's easy to get along with and easy to talk to. Career minded, goal oriented, driven and focused.

"Girl he makes six figures and he's single. He could be your new baby daddy ".

Women saying, "Look at her husband, he's so good to her and the kids". "They're so in love". He's head of his department and got a good benefits package. "Girl they went to Hawaii on their anniversary". Her parents just love him.

"Girl what's going on with Karen? She doesn't seem to be as happy as she used to be". "Have you noticed her husband doesn't really come around much anymore"? "They've been having problems for quite some time now. She mentioned he might be seeing someone else. But didn't have any real proof; but girl just a gut feeling. You know what I mean"?

As you know or have probably heard; friends, family members, co-workers and associates alike all talk like this. From the summer time corporate picnics and Christmas parties to weekend getaways with close friends.This is the conversation that's buzzing in the air just about always. But you still might be a little too young to hear about it firsthand. So I'll tell you everything I've heard over the years here.

Down low brothers have been around for years and they're not just associated with one group or race of people. They are everywhere. I'm not talking about the flamboyant and colorful "hey girlfriend" type that's going to get his nails and hair done. Or the guy whose looking at the men you're interested in wishing and hoping he's got a chance too.

I'm talking about "Mr. Well put together" and "Mr. Model man" masquerading throughout the city as

a metro sexual. It's not always him. Sometimes the ordinary man has a deep dark secret that only a select few know about. But none the less all these guys belong to a secret society of some sort where they meet and connect to socialize in their hidden but public clicks.

Make no mistake my daughter I'm not a subject matter expert by no means in this area. I'm only bringing it to light because over the years I've heard so many women say "I didn't know. I suspected something; but I didn't know". And in the end they were damaged and hurt. Other women never talk about it or share it with anyone else. They walk around in a secret shame. I do not have anything against homosexuality or gay rights. But be careful my daughter because these men are something else. They remain hidden in relationships with women, and are married with children and lead normal lives. But they mess with other men behind closed doors and parties and function in everyday life like any other man but there is a difference. These men enjoy hanging out with the guys and don't mind being penetrated.

I also imagine some of these men that go in and out of prison for lengthy periods of time have sex on the inside and on the outside. And in the grand scheme of things one hole is probably just as good as another. I'm not saying this for all x convicts but I would guess there's probably some truth to it.

My daughter this is not really something I want to talk about or even feel comfortable with. But you need to know. If he's excited about taking you from behind or just through casual conversations you find that anal sex is his thing you need to be cautious.

Follow your women's intuition and know that these men are out there and they do exist. If something doesn't feel right be prepared to walk away. Better yet, run.

Personal Boundaries
And making Men Respect You

There once was an older lady, whom I did not know, who shared some of her most private and traumatic little secrets with me about her life. She shared with me that she was raped several times in her life and twice by the same guy. She was fondled and unwillingly participated in a sexual encounter on her job which made her so uncomfortable that she quit. And how she struggled to raise her two kids without any financial help nor emotional support knowing they were from the men that raped her.

She went on to tell me how these events ruined her life and that she felt like what happened to her was partially her fault.

Charges were never pressed because she never reported the incidents. She never confronted the men. She just waited for it to eventually all just go away. She told me her kids were fairly young and that she hoped nothing like this would ever happen to them.

My daughter, know that sometimes situations get out of hand and go way too far. People get disrespected, hurt emotionally and physically because of the nature of the problem people sometimes have to call 911. And sometimes people have to go to jail.

In understanding personal boundaries know that you have to set boundaries in order to govern and protect you first and far most and to control how people interact with you.

Here are a few examples to get you thinking:

My daughter you have to first respect yourself and expect people to respect you. Accept nothing less. You always have the right to say no and nobody can force you to do anything you don't want to without there being consequences. No one can change you unless you let them; but always be the best person you can be. Never let anyone invade you space against your will and that includes your purse, phone, car or other personal belongings. Tell them get your hands off my stuff! Never tolerate abuse and if you don't feel like having company at your place you don't have to. If you already have plans don't let someone else break them. And lastly, if it's your television time and you don't feel like being interrupted then don't be. People will have you jumping all over the place at their beck and call if you don't learn this early.

I recall dating a lady I went to college with for a short period of time. She was fun, she was nice and I enjoyed hanging out with her for a while. But after nearly nine months or so I came to the conclusion that she and I were not a good fit. In various conversations prior, she told me how she damaged a few guys property due to bad breakups. Slashing tires and furniture as well as breaking out windows made her feel better before she moved on. We eventually broke up and it was my decision. Of course she didn't take it well. She drove by my apartment off and on periodically calling, cursing and occasionally catching me in the parking lot and embarrassing me in front of other tenants. Until one day she saw me with my coworker. It was my turn. My windshield, passenger door, antenna and both front tires. That was her grand exit and the relationship was officially over in her eyes. As I stood there in awe with a dumb look on my face not knowing what to do. My coworker suggested that I call the cops. Long story short, police showed up, I pressed charges, she went to jail, towed her car, I never saw her again.

After this incident I learned to tell women up front I will call the police. Ironically, I have never experienced anything else like this again.

Having personal boundaries will help you manage situations as they come up and allow you to protect yourself before things get out of hand. Understand, being firm will let people know exactly how far they can go. And they will think twice.

Now that you've set some boundaries it's time to make sure men respect you. Know that men who lie have to say goodbye. If he can't respect and treat you nice you shouldn't date him. If he's easily angered and verbally abusive get away quick because he might decide to put his hands on you. Don't stick around to find out. If he takes anything from you without asking he's stealing and that's not cute. Get rid of him too. And lastly, if you see him or suspect him of dating other women while

he's in a relationship with you for a fact, kick him to the curb. It only gets worse.

While dating always require a man to treat you like a lady. He should open every door, pull your seat out to seat you first, pay the check most of the time and pursue you. If he's not doing these things and you're running after him know that it's because someone else has his interest. And you're the side chick. After all, he would expect another guy to treat his sister like this.

When you require your expectations to be met, you'll see, he'll go above and beyond for you because he wants to show you he could possibly be the one. If he's not going to meet your requirements chances are he'll fizzle out and lose interest around date number two or three if you're doing it right and that's good. It beats having someone tell you they're moving on after ten or twelve months because they lost interest around the six month mark and they were hoping you went away.

Again, I can't say it enough. You are precious and your time is valuable. Don't let men waste it because you never get it back. Don't let men monopolize your time especially if they're just there to play.

And never let anybody do anything to you nor your body or force you to do something against your will without telling someone who can help you and protect you. And lastly, sometimes you have to make a person understand that you mean what you mean.

Don't be afraid to fight there are real men out there who will help you in a stressful situation. But remember fight to keep him off of you. Don't go chasing him out the door or through the parking lot and down the street only to get beat up. I see so many women doing this holding their eye and screaming why did he hit me. It's simple, because he was defending himself.

Never start a physical fight with a man you will sure lose in most cases. You may cut him up with your mouth; but if you provoke him to raise his fist you still lose. Know when enough is enough and walk away. Better yet be the lady who learns to not get caught up with men like this.

Rules to dating
And spending the night

Are there rules to dating? My daughter you better believe it! The rules are spoken, unspoken, publicly talked about and kept in secret. Rules change from person to person and whether you're a man or a boy a woman or a girl if you date you will play "the game". Learn the rules, make the rules, follow the rules, understand the rules and know rules can and will be broken.

So what are the rules? There are many rules but I'll run down a few you need to know. Some men say "never fall in love" or "never commit". I've known women to say "I never kiss on the first date or he has to ask me out at least three time before I agree to go". One of my personal rules has always been a woman has to pick up the check occasionally. The number one rule to dating is this... until you feel totally comfortable hanging around him meet him out. Usually this day in time people live further away from each other so it's more acceptable to meet at mutual locations. Besides, inviting someone into your private space is considered a big step. Take your time there's no rush. You should really get to know him first and at least know his real name if he uses a nick name like "Lil Red" or "Big Tycoon". It wouldn't hurt to know a little background on him either. I once dated a lady that waited 6 months before she invited me over. I was only invited over once and I never saw her again. I really wasn't interested in her. We were never intimate. She protected herself very well. I respected her very much for that. Learn to make some decisions with your head and not your heart because you'll be a lot better off. Never compromise how you feel especially if you're feeling uncomfortable.

When it comes to dating don't assume anything. Let him say it. Wait for him to tell you what he's thinking and what's going on in his mind unless his actions are clearly speaking louder than his words. And then, you should probably proceed with caution and check for consistency. Because if he's buying you flowers, telling you he loves you, not taking your calls at night and sending other phone calls to voicemail when he is with you something smells a little fishy.

Know that women often push guys into relationships or into saying those three little words long before they get to that point. And what do guys do? They go along with it. The girl says "I love you". The guy says "yep uh huh". The girl says do you love me? Then he says "uh huh".

And at that point the girl is in a committed loving relationship. At least in her mind, she has begun to invest her heart. She starts giving her body to him and that's fine because that's really what he wanted. She starts introducing him to her friends and he's feeling the friend more than her. Six months later, girlfriend is sad and her heart is broken because her boyfriend turned out to be no good.

In his mind he was still getting to know her and they were, that's right, "JUST FRIENDS". Men get in relationships to see where it's going to go.

Men ask women out on Monday for a date on Friday then Sometimes won't call till Friday 1 hour before the date or not at all.

If this happens always cancel that date or don't bother to take his call. It's important that you know If a man is truly interested in you he's going to touch basis with you throughout the week leading up to the date. If he's not calling you he's not interested and don't bother trying to force anything because usually the girl ends up hurt.

Dating one on one should always have a purpose. I recommend hanging out in groups with friends because it "should be" less stressful and less likely to end up somewhere you don't really want to be. In this environment dating is somewhat controlled. For example, meeting up at a bowling alley with four or five friends is a great fun date. Now days there are mega arcades that usually have a great deal of stuff to do that are fun and exciting. When going to a show being in a group or double dating is a good way to go as well. **Beware of friends that try to convince you to have sex with a guy; or in this day in age a group.**

While dating, relationships progress from hugging, to holding hands, to kissing and touching to eventually sex and spending the night. As your father I wish no guy, you hear me, no guy, would ever spend the night with you nowhere. All I'm going to say is this. You need to really know him and be sure you can trust him. I would recommend being in a serious committed monogamous relationship and waiting at least one year minimum before he spends the night. You should know that spending the night could end up in disaster. If he leaves at 3-4 o'clock in the morning or does not call the next day you should know in most cases he doesn't want you.

If you just so happen to have a guy friend and it's platonic or if he's honestly gay and he sleeping on the sofa that might be okay. But if it's anything other than that just know your eyes better be wide open and you better be ready. Spending the night leads to sex willingly and sometimes against your will. I'm not saying it doesn't happen because you and I both know better. And if it were left up to me, you would

have to wait. He would have to wait for you. Every daughter should wait and make him wait because what you don't know is that he'll respect you. And in the end appreciate you for making him wait.

The key is to wait and make him wait. You'll be better off for it. He'll be better off and

believe it or not he'll appreciate you in the long run.

My Daughter the Significant Other Or just a Booty Call

My daughter, know that men put women into only two categories marriage material and not marriage material. We call it several different things and look at it several different ways; but in the end either he will or won't marry you. Understand because you need to know this determines the outcome of the relationship and the direction it goes in. I've seen men date women for 5, 6, sometimes 7, or 8 years only to breakup with them or move on later. Men have children from women they don't want. But to put it politically correct women have children from men who don't want them. A man will break up with a woman then meet someone else and within 1-2 years he could marry that woman.

Men date for the enjoyment and to blow time. We also date to marry; but in most cases that comes a little later. I'm telling you this because it gets complicated and you need to know this. The last thing you want to do is have your heart entangled with a man who does not want you. It's hurtful, it's embarrassing;

but there's nothing you can do about it. As a father speaking I'm saying be cautious.

Let me back up for a minute and just say for the record that I do know several guys that have met girls in their early teenage years and married them early and are still married. I think that's beautiful. Marriage is beautiful and children are a blessing. I'm telling you this because you need to know the truth. When you look around and see men with women and boys with girls. You can always ask yourself does he love her and is he willing to marry her. Then look at you own relationship. I personally know that people date and enter relationships for the time being and the feelings mutual. I also know people get involved when they don't love; but for other reasons. I'm merely pointing all this out because whatever the reason is for coming together make sure you know his purpose and visa-versa.

In your relationship are you going to be the significant other or just a booty call?

If you're the significant other he's going to spend and invest his resources with you and plant seeds into your lives as they intertwine together. Life and love in most cases will move and grow in the same directions. The possibility of them slowly and eventually becoming one is very likely. This relationship stands the possibility of being very promising and beautiful.

Now on the other hand when it comes to Miss Booty Call it's going to be very different. She's not his significant other. No matter how much time they spend together, in his mind, she's temporary. And in most cases they meet up or see each other here any there. The encounters are mainly sexual and there's very few emotions. Booty calls use to be late night creeps going to see someone just for sex; but now the time of day don't really matter and the frequency has increased. It's really hard to tell them apart.

If you're the significant other you'll meet family. He will take your calls. He'll want to exchange Christmas and birthday gifts with you and spend holidays together. He'll take pictures and post on social media with you. He'll be there for you in every way. You won't be a secret. The key is exchange. Men receive gifts from women who care as often as they can get them.

There's nothing else to say about Miss Booty Call except in most cases he'll see you when he see you and you'll know who you are. But be careful because sometimes he'll keep that a secret even from you. In other words Miss Booty Call might not know her own name.

Here's a hint for you. **If he has a problem with you popping up at his place just know it's because he doesn't let anyone pop up. It means he has more than one woman.** Don't fall for, I go to bed early on Tuesdays and turn the ringer off at 8:00pm. Or some other weird story. If it sounds far fetch it's because it is.

Making babies

My daughter I'm not going to say a whole lot about making babies; but I will say this. Babies are wonderful gifts from God that come into this world bringing joy and happiness under normal circumstances and should be created out of love. They should never be unwanted, abused or thrown away.

This day in age everybody got a baby by somebody. No husband and have never been married. I'll

tell any young lady without a husband not to get pregnant. In most cases her life will be ruined or made extremely difficult and that guy is not going to be there. And if he ever decides to get married just know it's not to the girl he had a baby with at the age of seventeen or twenty one nor even twenty four or twenty seven as a matter of fact. So I strongly suggest you keep your legs closed. But if you find out that you just can't or don't want to, always make him use condoms for your protection or get on some long term type birth control. You may not understand or get it now but I promise in five or ten years you'll be glad you did it. And if a boy whispers in your ear he loves you and wants you to have his baby tell him heck no. If you're twenty five years old or older with a ring on your finger that's a different story go ahead and have your baby.

As best as you can make plans and preparations to have a baby with someone you love and respect who love and cherish you.Who plans to be there long term like "your husband". And even after that, if you could wait until you're somewhat financially **stable starting a family is a wonderful thing.**

I can count hundreds of situations where I've met young girls around your age with children. They all had that same glossy look in their eyes. From the grocery store line where they're short on money and having to put something back; to working their job at some fast food restaurant at 1:00am in the morning. That look in their eyes is a look of no hope and abandonment. Robbed of their innocence and feeling all alone I'm pleading with you to avoid this because it doesn't have to be you.

There are other situations that are less costly. I'd rather see you get caught up in a bad hair style or dye you have to live with for a month or so. Or the new guy that just started calling; you find out that he's a real dog before he get to dogging you. These are situations you find yourself in and get out. Not a baby though. Diapers, formula, and clothes are all things a baby need every day. There goes that little pay check. You need a baby sitter. Got to pay for daycare. Uh oh! Where is he? He who? Your baby daddy! I don't know. Now you're going to struggle and do this by yourself. But guess what? You just met a real nice guy this morning. Uh oh again, sounds like baby number two to me.

I'm not wishing this for you at all. I'm just painting a couple of pictures and telling a few stories hoping you can catch on.

Babies, abusive relationships and men you got to take care of because they working you over in the bedroom are all situations you need to avoid early in life. But if you're single and financially stable when you reach thirty five and got one of the pretty eyed men with good hair and abs handling up in the bedroom then that's your business. I probably won't say a word. I'll just shake my head when you're not looking.

Shacking Versus getting A Ring

My daughter understand part of defining and knowing who you are will have a direct correlation with how you live and what your values are in life. From choosing which boy to exchange phone numbers with to that special someone you kiss know that it's your choice.

Boys, men, guys or whatever you decide to call them at this point they'll all play a part in your life when it comes to dating. And when things decide to get a little serious know that the conversation of living arrangements will usually come up. So in this situation know that you have two choices. You can choose to shack or you can hold out to get a ring. I won't make this long and boring but know that in most cases men that will shack with you are really just there temporarily. They think you're beautiful, smart, and got it going on. All the while feeling like they can do better than you and just waiting for a better opportunity to come along. He'll stay for six months or six years. He might and probably will give you a baby or two. Along the way you might even meet his girlfriend. Wait a minute, you're the girlfriend! This happens every day to thousands of women all over the country. She's in a happy committed relationship or at least she thought she was. When his mess hit the fan and his lies and deceit finally catch up to him he will gladly pack his stuff and part of yours too and go shack somewhere else.

Don't get me wrong I've seen men and women live together and eventually get married even after he's had children, girlfriends on the side, fights and jail time. I'm not saying it's impossible. The likelihood of this working is slim.

To sum everything up, shacking will in most cases get your feelings hurt and lead to you being unhappy. And you know I want you to be happy.

Now when it comes to getting the ring know that if you are exactly what he's looking for and his life is somewhat remotely together he'll marry you. And it's just that simple. Understand and know that simply **put men marry who they want.**

To break this down almost scientific like know that men categorize, rate, evaluate and eliminate women. But don't panic! I just need you to know so you know what you're up against. Look around you see men and women married all over the place. Notice some of them make cute couples and some of them don't and in reality all that don't even matter. I'm going to tell you why right here. **What men value varies from man to man.**

Here's the example: A rapper will value his rhymes, and athlete his athletic abilities and a business man his intellect and savvy. And they all make millions but their values are different.

So if you're beautiful, slim, tall, and smart dating a guy who like beautiful, thick, short and dumb chances are he's not going to marry you. Your best friend is short, dark complexioned, full figured and beautiful with short hair. She's trying to figure why he won't marry her after two years and she's tired and frustrated with the relationship because it's not going anywhere. She should know it's because she's not the one for him. He's really into thin, fair skinned women with big butts and long hair.

But if by chance she meet a guy who like short, pretty and black she'll stand a better chance because she's actually what he's looking for.

Now, let's move on a little further. She's what he likes on the outside. She's got a pretty smile and everything. She's even easy to talk to and fun to spend time with. As they get to know each other over time he finds out she's educated with a good job and got her own place and no kids. Guess what she like him too. You hear the wedding bells? **Because she just got the ring.**

But what if she had a stank attitude, and frowned up whenever discussions didn't go her way and walked off in the middle of conversations getting angry and not answering the phone for days. Know that there's a great possibility he's going to move on even if he really doesn't want to.

Understand men have a checklist that go like this. She's tall, too tall, short, too short, too thick, and she's just right. Pretty, not pretty enough. She's dark, and she's too dark. Now, what offsets this list are assets or good qualities such as personable, smart, education, income, cooking ability, so on and so forth the list goes on.

But it's not real long because men are not complicated creatures. So off the long list each man is only going to have a few things he's looking for. It boils down to his likes, unexpected extras, dislikes and what he has to have.

You could meet your ideal man and fall head over hills in love. But he has to have a high yellow woman, with hazel eyes and a rap video body. If he can get her he might take her being jobless with three kids and an unpleasant attitude. You on the other hand could bring to the table all the extras like a great personality, good job and no kids and a college degree. You've planned the perfect wedding and trying to save your money waiting for him to propose. But he won't do it because you're not the one.

Inquire about what's on his list and his values. He has an ideal woman and be honest with yourself. If you don't fit know that it's not going work. Also know that as men get older their preferences and values change.

Women make relationships and dating way to complicated for themselves by going for the man that don't want them and pushing away that guy who does. I'm not saying marry a frog; but if the frog is on the list take a second look at him. Let me

say this one more time. **If you're not on his list he is not going to turn you down. He's just not going to marry you.**

Talk Shows
And Reality TV

This day in age television reality shows are more popular than they have ever been. From dysfunctional families to sex, drugs, and washed up celebrities you can find just about anything on television at any time. Just because it's reality television doesn't mean it has to be your reality. All the shows are geared for ratings but none the less they have truths and they share lessons to be learned if you pay attention.

I personally don't watch reality television but I believe if you do, educate yourself while you're being entertained. Learn what to do and what not to do and why. Pay attention to how certain situations get blown out of hand. If you choose to date him knowing he's cheating expect the drama. Baby daddy and momma drama, fighting over a man, and just being ratchet is no way to conduct yourself in your everyday life.

Being strung out on drugs and prostitution is no way to live because you don't have to. Be careful because people get caught up and introduced to pornography and all sorts of stuff. It's hard to escape when you're pressured and forced into these types of life changing habits.

Not knowing whose the father and being baby momma number five are all situations to make sure you don't get caught up in. In addition to this you find tons of makeup and exotic hair.

Pink, blue and green hair is absolutely no way to go on a job interview, go to work, or be seen in public. Don't get me wrong some of it is nice; but when it's extreme it's distasteful and sends the wrong message. Please don't get half of your hair shaved bald because you saw it on a million dollar super star whose on the cover of a magazine. If you can't maintain the hair style please don't get it.

Tattoos are not a huge deal to me. I personally don't have any myself because I just decided not to. Over the years I've been drawn to women who have them. One or two, three or four and sometimes a couple more. But again, not when they're distasteful or in the wrong places like the face or neck, hands and wrists; or on your calf area. But on the other hand the women I've seriously dated over the years usually had very few; or none at all.

Don't get me wrong I've seen men tatted up all over including the neck and sometimes face too with their boos looking just like them. I'm not saying it's impossible to have a career with tattoos all over your body I'm just saying think it through. When I was younger I had a couple of bosses whom I respected very much. They wore suits to work every day and carried themselves in a very professional manner. One day during break time one of them just so happened to come to the job while on vacation. He was tatted up from an inch above the wrist to the shoulders on both arms but you couldn't tell and probably would have never guessed. It's important to know if you got to have them make sure they can be covered.

Men Versus Boys

What makes a man, a man; and what makes a boy a boy? Look at these three areas and they will tell you plenty about what you need to know to determine if he's a man or a boy. His outlook on life and how he chooses to live it will show you plenty about him so pay close attention. His ability to handle situations responsibly and his level of maturity will carry him along way.

When examining these areas with any guy you must ask yourself the question; Why? Why did he do that? Why did he say that? Why did he ignore me? Why, why, why. Now when it comes to relationships this is going to be very important because whether you're dating a man or a boy you need to understand the differences between the two and how they're going to think.

For the record men will usually be more mature emotionally, more stable and grounded when it comes to their career and have more awareness about their appearances. They're going to have plans and set goals to get where they want to be.

On the other hand boys are usually just the opposite. In some instances a boy will wear his feelings on his sleeve and in his pants. He might even be just as moody as your best girlfriend. He's not grounded, poor work ethics and working history; plans and goals are unfamiliar to him as well.

Now, when it comes to relationships men are going to be straight forward regardless of what they want from you. They are sure of themselves and usually won't waste to much time beating around the bush.

You might be taken with his directness. But if he's remotely interested in you, or not, he's going to make it known. This is why you see women at the age of 25 or 30 dating or married to men 10, 15, and even 20 years older and are in very beautiful and fulfilling relationship. But on the other hand you also see firsthand or hear stories where the girl whose 20,25 years old is pregnant or already has a child or two from an older guy who just so happens to be married. And for the record he's not leaving his wife. Know that men also sometimes act like boys and in certain aspects never change.

Boys will usually lie about what they have or what they had. In their earlier ages their priorities are partying, sex, cars, music, and yeah that about sums it up. They make babies accidentally caught up in the moment with the wrong girl. They live life totally unpredictably and by doing so become very predictable and you know their behaviors soon become non-surprising.

After reading this it's starting to sound a little confusing I know. But go back to the beginning. Always look at the three things above because they'll tell you just about everything. So now let's clarify. Some men are actually still boys and some boys are actually mature men.

Her are two examples that are true. In my later twenties when I was in real estate I met a kid. I call him a kid because of his age only. He was interested in buying a home for his family I showed him a small starter home because I knew that was all he could afford.

He looked to have been about 20 or so and his girlfriend couldn't have been more than eighteen or nineteen.

He wouldn't buy that starter home. Needless to say he proved me wrong all the way around. That was his wife and kid. He had been in love with her since Jr. High. He married her after Senior high school right after he got a good job where he was working his way up. They planned their family and bought the biggest house. Over a couple of years I watched them plan and make moves to furnish their home, buy new cars, and vacation. In my eyes this guy is a man. Off and on over the years we've run into each other. Life has not always been roses; but I've watched him make good decisions, use sound judgment and develop and follow his plans and make sacrifices.

Now on the other hand I had a neighbor who was in his sixties and was retired. He wore FUBU gear, if you don't know what that is, look it up, gold chains and all the latest swag at that time. He had a grandpa car that he parked on the curb and a SUV with rims that he washed in the driveway with the music up loud on the weekends. He watched rap videos, smoked, drank, and ran old women like they were all in their twenties and wishing he could catch a young sweet tender. He cursed and talked plenty of trash. The only thing he didn't do was wear his pants sagging with his butte out and his underwear showing. He was his own man and just being him.

I can go on and on with examples. Men and boys cheat, get drunk, use drugs, mismanage money, hit women, go to jail, and the list goes on and on. But you need to look at his standards and beliefs for himself. How does he live his life, does he handle situations responsibly, and is he mature or immature. Nobody is perfect; but I'm sure you'd rather end up with a guy who loves you, goes to work and contribute to the home and spends time with his kids versus and abusive drunk who cheats and stay gone for days at a time.

This day in age I see so many young guys walking around with their pants hanging off their buttes and clothes two sizes too big with $500.00 worth of clothes on standing on the bus stop and his girlfriend's outfit came from the 7 dollar store. They got a baby and the young mother's life is ending before it really ever started and she doesn't know it.

You see, she's working every day to take care of him and her mom is working and helping her take care of her baby and grandma babysits. What is he doing? He's doing absolutely nothing at home playing video games and running the streets.

The Art of making good Decisions And Mastering Perception

My daughter every day of your life situations will arise. Whether it's school, work, spending time with your boyfriend or partying and staying out all night you will need to make decisions. And your decisions will need to be good ones. Good decisions lead to good and favorable outcomes and opportunities. Bad decisions have repercussions and consequences.

Two identical twins are going to the same college party. One twin stays a few hours because she has work and class the next day she's back home and in bed at 12:00am. The other twin stays later and at 1:00am she drunk and smoking marijuana. At 2:00am she's in a bedroom with 3 other girls and 5 guys. Back at home her sister wakes up at 7:00am to get ready for class only to find that twin never made it home. She calls her sister's cell phone; but there's no answer. Later that day when she returns home from school, work and the library she sees her sister laid in bed. A couple of months later her sister leaves school because she's pregnant.

I remember when I was in my early twenties I had a job working at the phone company. Our next door neighbor worked there for over 25 years when she told me about it and pointed me in that direction. You see the "phone company" was one of those places where people went to work for 30-40 years and retired happy and without any financial problems.

She told me exactly where to go and what day to go on because during this time you pretty much had to know somebody. I took the test and passed. The lady let me know someone would be calling me in 6-8 weeks. I didn't get a phone call so I went and got a good job working at the vacuum store. A few months later I saw my neighbor again and she asked me did I like working at the "phone company". I told her I didn't work there, and she said, "Why not! You passed the test! You need to go get your job"!

At that moment I thought she was crazy so I just said ok and went on my way. A few weeks later I went back to the testing center and after waiting for almost one and a half hours I was taking to the back.

I spoke with a lady and then a second lady. After a little longer a third lady came in and told me that there was an oversight on their part and there was a job available. She said, "It's probably not going to be something you're interested in but if you like the training class starts on Monday".

After she told me I probably wasn't going to be interested I quickly made my decision without hesitating. She told me there were just a few papers I needed to sign and that she would be right back because they had already waist to much of my time.

Within seconds after she left a different lady rushed in and out really quick. But while she was there she said while whispering, "Don't let them do that to you. You better take that job. Don't let them do that to you". Then she disappeared.

The lady came back in smiling with paperwork in hand and when I told her I had a change in heart she became very disappointed. Needless to say within a blink of the eye it seemed I had been there over a year and was near top pay for that position which was almost $7.00 more than where I started. With full medical, dental vacation pay, holiday pay, sick pay, flexible days and 401k. It was clear to me how people worked there for 25 plus years.

Now moving forward another six months I started having difficulties with my supervisors and managers and abruptly from one day to the next I quit. I walked away and never looked back. Twenty years later I still think about this. Because I realized later that I wasn't in control and I made my decisions based on limited knowledge, anger and frustrations.

Till this day my dad says that was the best Job I ever had. Now let's analyze. Did I exercise good judgment? Did I gather information needed to make a good decision? Did I use perception?

I ended up leaving the "phone company" and going to the "yellow pages" which was a subsidiary of the "phone company". And their benefits were good; but different and the money I made there was more than twice as much. Life was truly good. And about five years later I did a repeat meltdown. One to many things didn't go my way and I made another hasty decision to walk away. I found out several months later that the company had a retirement buyout with the employees who had been there for 25 plus years and the senior level jobs that were held by people with tenure all became available and filled within months and I missed it.

In my life I've made a countless number of poor decisions and in every aspect. From breaking up with my college girlfriend who went on to become a doctor, to divorcing my ex prematurely. Nah, I was ready to get out of that. There are hundreds more though that I dare not talk about because they were just dumb and idiotic.

I once saw and old friend at a party. To my recollection I knew he was a drinker and the life of the party. This particular night I was puzzled because he was not drinking. As the night progressed and most guys were tipsy of course he was not. We eventually talked and of course I asked him why he was not drinking. His response was, "When I drink I do dumb stuff". And I'm just paraphrasing. Part of making good decision and mastering perception is not to make the same mistakes over and over and having some idea what the outcome is going to be.

When it comes to making good decisions and mastering perception I will say this. First, think things through before making a decision by weighing the pros and cons. Second, as often as possible, talk with someone who is not heavily connected to your life then someone who is. And lastly, look into your future at the possible outcomes. There are always several possible outcomes so you have to explore each one. Get good at this and minimize poor decisions. You'll find yourself further ahead in life with less stress and drama.

Anticipating Outcomes

My daughter, know that everything you do creates a response or a reaction. Be cautious because situations become explosive and get out of hand very quickly. I've seen family members hanging out and having a nice time in one moment and then fighting, threatening to do bodily harm and kill the next. All because somebody said something wrong at the wrong time. If you're not involved in the situation directly avoid being pulled into it at all cost. And if it's not a very close friend or family member don't you go jumping into it!

Know that everything in life usually follows a course. The student that studies hard and does their work throughout the school year makes good grades and will usually graduate. The person that goes to college and apply themselves and focus will usually graduate and start a nice career and so on and so forth.

Know that on any job performance and accuracy are noted. If a person under perform continuously they'll be looking another job fairly soon.

I saw on a show once, a man had been cheating on his wife for a couple of years and had a baby by another woman. He brought his wife onto the show to apologize, and ask for forgiveness. Once he told his wife everything, she starting crying hysterically and yelled out she was filing for divorce. The man became hurt, upset and angry because his wife of 8 years was leaving him and taking their children.

Crazy! I know. The man should have known that if his wife found out he was out cheating there was a great possibility that she would leave him.

In short, unprotected sex leads to making babies, abortions, diseases, having to fight with someone else's significant other, and possibly death. Having a job that doesn't pay enough money leads to struggling, lights being turned off, not enough food, not being able to pay rent, getting evicted and living in the streets. Being in and abusive relationship, using drugs, being a single mother, and choosing a life of crime all have their own unique courses.

So does going to college, hanging in when the job gets a little tuff and being found by the right somebody and raising a family. Starting a business is tuff; but with the right mindset and a few extra ingredients along the way it can lead to financial freedom and most of your dreams coming true.

The young woman sitting in church with 3 little kids beside her and one in her belly without a husband was once a virgin. And the young man facing 25 years in prison for rape was a star college football player, star high school athlete, junior high super star, little league starter and the apple of his dad's eye.

This chapter is here to open you mind so you can start visualizing the outcomes and situations that will come up in your life. The cake on the box is there so you can see how the ingredients mixed together along with the instructions come together.

Simply put start with the end result in mind. Before you lay on your back.... Think. Chances are, in all honesty he's not going to want you. If you take something out of the store without paying for it chances are you will get caught and end up with a record that will keep you from working a nice job for a very long time.

Having a good Attitude Is key

In life having a good attitude will determine how far you go, how fast you get there and how hard the road in life will be. Your attitude is the key that will unlock doors that might ordinarily be closed to you. And on the other hand if it's bad, doors will shut in your face and people that could possibly and easily help make a difference on your behalf will not budge to do so.

When I think back on my life I remember being told on several occasions that I had a bad attitude. I first noticed that something that could be affected by my attitude was my conduct grades in school and then later in life.

When I was in the fifth grade I specifically remember getting in trouble and being punished at home all because I had poor conduct grades that year.

I recall having a "C" for conduct and being punished for a whole six weeks period. I couldn't go outside and play on school days. For the next six weeks I did not say a word to anybody in class because I was determined to not be punished again. I held my tongue and deliberately became the little dumb and mute kid who couldn't talk and wouldn't talk.

I wanted to make my momma proud of her little boy by getting at least a "B". When that report card came out I had another dreaded "C". It got so bad I remember changing my grade. Later the teacher saw and told me; "If you would have had a "B" this six weeks then you would have had a "B" for every six weeks. I realized then that my conduct grade wasn't going to change no matter how hard I tried and for the whole year it remained the same.

When I got to junior high I played basked ball and I was kind of like a super star. I remember having a fall out with the coach because I got angry and disobeyed a direct order. Even though I was one of the better players on the team I was the only one that didn't get a trophy that year. I noticed something was wrong when the kids that didn't really get to play much got trophies too.

I went on to high school. I was older and more mature. The coach told my dad I had a bad attitude and my dad told me. Of course I disagreed. Long story short I didn't play much in high school.

Starting to see the picture? I always had a teacher here and there that liked me usually because I liked them. Strange I know; but it gets even more interesting.

I graduated high school and my teacher got me a job at a bank. After I got there I met a guy that was a few years older than me. I'll call him Supercool Attitude. Shortly after meeting him I didn't like him; but I found out very quickly that everyone else at the bank did.

I found out I was hired so he didn't have to be the only guy working with all the ladies. I also found out that without any experience they let him become a commercial teller because he wanted to give it a try. When he didn't like it; but did a great job any way they promoted him to new accounts.

Later that year he bought a sports car and I remember walking through the bank with him one Friday evening after closing time.The bank president asked him why he didn't buy another particular sports car that was quite a bit more expensive. He explained the monthly payments were too high.

I remember hearing the bank president say "Ah Supercool Attitude we would have worked the payments where you could have afforded them". My mouth hit the floor. Within twelve months this guy was a loan officer working in the bank being trained by the other loan officer who was probably twice his age and a dozen shades lighter.

I was being written up for under performance and needless to say at year end I didn't get a raise. And I was off looking for another job.

I saw Supercool Attitude about 6 years later. I was excited to see him and anxious to hear where he was working. He told me same place and that he was a branch manager. For years this particular bank only had one branch. They opened a second and put him in charge. His attitude was his key to his success that opened all the doors.

For some people having a good attitude will come naturally and for others it takes time and hard work to develop. It is a skill that can be learned and mastered. Remember rain or shine always smile. Being pleasant is a must. Kind words and laughter will always carry you far. Learn this early in life because **your attitude will make the biggest difference in your life.**

Sometimes things
Just don't make sense

Sometimes while driving on the freeway you may notice it's pouring rain and the windshield wipers are going full speed then suddenly it's not raining. Twenty five yards further it's raining hard again. It's hot today then cold tomorrow and sometimes hot and cold in the same day.

Thinking about someone prompts a phone call from that person or you actually run into them. You see grass growing on the concrete. College graduates are jobless and living with their parents. School teachers involved sexually with their students. You see all these things happening and yes sometimes things just don't make sense.

Keep moving forward in life my daughter. Don't be afraid to make mistakes. Never be afraid to make changes or to start over. Life is a journey you just have to take it and know that you can accomplish anything you put your mind to. Don't start over to much though, because of unnecessary mistakes. They will always keep you in a situation of lack and struggle.

Sometimes you see people that do everything right end up with so much going wrong and people doing everything wrong appear to have so much good fortune. This is only temporary. It comes to an end when they least expect it.

Always remember my daughter. The key is to always try to find the good in everybody and do right or good as often as possible. Be a giver and give more than you receive. Think positive thoughts every day. Focus hard on your needs and wants and watch what God does. Always dream big and learn to speak your positive thoughts out loud. And lastly be prepared for change and know that change is growth. It is uncomfortable; but necessary.

Roll with the punches. Take a few and give a few. Never back down and never give up. If need be go around. There's always another way to get to where you want to be. Be smart my daughter, sometimes it's just best to be still and wait.

Being independent
And preparing for rainy days

My daughter I think from the time I was 19 or 20 years old I don't recall getting much help financially from anyone. I pretty much had to manage things on my own and with very little guidance and I made a bunch of mistakes. One good thing was I lived at home with my parents so I had free rent at least for a few years after I graduated. Don't get me wrong my parents were there for me. I just felt like I was finally grown and wanted to be on my own as much as possible. My daughter I was wrong, communication with your parents, and any positive older role model or friend is important.

This day in age young adults move out of their parent's house far earlier than they should. They're unprepared due to growing up in broken homes, instabilities and maturing way to fast; and often moving with a boyfriend and, or a baby. My daughter, know that struggling on your own with very little help is tuff and that you will need a game plan. So first, **scratch the boyfriend and the baby at least for 3-5 years because right now you don't need either one. I promise you will be far ahead of your peers with boyfriends and or kids. It's ok to date; but don't necessarily obligate yourself to someone especially if you kind of feel like he's just temporary. Trust me you'll know.**

Being independent means just that. When a person is independent they can usually manage on their own. Paying your own bills, living by yourself and making your own decisions usually constitute being independent. For the record self-sustained people have an income. They will go to work, have their own money, live by themselves or with a roommate, grocery shop for themselves and pay their own bills. Usually they will make their own decisions. **Being independent pretty much mean being**

responsible for one's own self. It doesn't mean you're not going to have problems; but in most cases you should be in a position to handle them on your own. So, when it comes to getting a job avoid jobs that just won't pay the bills. Examples are fast food chains, retail establishments, grocery stores and cashier type jobs. This is only assuming you're not in college at this time; or it's referring to someone who decided not to go to college. Non the less just be smart about your job search. Also know that the jobs and industries I just eliminated are not for you now; but later we will pick this back up in another chapter.

Here's a nugget for you to think about. There are two waitresses working with the same amount of experience and both working at seafood restaurants. The one with a horrible attitude works in a very nice upscale part of town and the other has a great personality and works near a college campus. Which one do you think will make the most money? Correct, probably the girl with the horrible attitude because it's not totally based on her abilities alone.

Remember the story where I worked at a bank? One of my high school classmates came through the drive thru to cash his pay check one day. I noticed his pay for a two week period was twice that of mine. As a bank teller

I gained customer service and cash handling experience there and made $5.00 per hour. Later, I took the experience and worked for the telephone company and made three times as much. And about 10 years later I took that same skill set and polished it up and went to work for a local home builder and made over 100k per year.

While working for the home builder I met an older gentleman that was in that industry for close to 30 years. Jobs pay differently based on industry. So be smart, do a little homework on the internet and ask questions. The path you choose will directly determine the money you will make. Money equates to nice things. Expensive shoes, purses, perfume, spa and beauty shop treatments, happy hour lunches, new cars, homes, apartments, vacations with your girlfriends and so much more. **I choose for you to not be broke, busted and disgusted! I'm speaking prosperity into your life right here.**

Being independent, working and making money is good but also part of being independent is preparing for rainy days.

What is a rainy day you might ask? A rainy day is just about any day that you did not prepare for and shows up unexpectedly. In life there are many types of rainy days. We have rainy days, rainy weeks, and rainy seasons that could last for years. Usually they'll mess your mood up and make you want to go yelling, screaming and ready to pull your hair out. Be calm because screaming and yelling does not help at all. A tire needing to be fixed or replaced is one example. Your car needing a brake job is another. But these are simple. Imagine your car making a strange noise and the mechanic says you need new pistons or a whole new motor because you hadn't changed the car oil in almost a year. Or, you're driving, and suddenly the smoke under the hood turns into fire and people are driving by while you're standing on side of the road. These issues are a little more serious.

Know that people experience job loss, thefts of property, damage that need replacing, health issues, auto, other type of accidents and a slew of other serious incidents and situations. Know that these types of incidents happen to people daily. So the best way to combat these issues are to be prepared as best as you can.

Save, save, save your money and hold on to it as best as possible! Pay yourself first. Get a 401k or some type of retirement account whenever offered. And if a company offers you stock options go for it.

Starting out there are several different methods you can use to save money that are simple. You can start by saving loose coins. Get a plastic juice jug and only save quarters. You'll be surprised when it's time for a new tire you'll have the money. Save all your coins for years and years or manage to save spare dollars if you can. In five or seven years you'll have a really good habit of saving and a nice little cushion. Out of all the saving tips the one I like best is a second banking account. Usually your bank will offer you a free checking account this day in time. When they do link it to your primary account and have $5.00 dollars a week or $10.00 - $20.00 or more per pay check automatically go into the other account. Forget about it no debit card or statement. But when you need it you'll be surprised.

I'm sharing this information with you now because I was nearly in my late twenties when I learned these valuable life lessons. The two things you must learn to manage are your time and your money.

Managing time is just what it is. I recall when I was younger my uncle would carry a to do list of things he needed to get done daily, weekly, and monthly.

Along the way he would add to the list and delete task as he completed them. He always had a time limit whenever he stopped to talk and always knew what he was doing next.

Set goals and work towards them. Goals could be daily, weekly, monthly, quarterly, yearly, 3, 5&10 years out. Always write them down and post them visibly where you can see them. Talk about them, make them realistic and strive to reach them. **Know that your goals will be your road map to help keep you focused to get you where you need to go.**

Struggling financially

My daughter I think at some point in life just about everyone struggles with something. Whether it's the loss of a loved one; or being forced to make an uncomfortable decision that just about changes everything, for whatever the reason, we all will find ourselves struggling with some sort of change. Welcomed or unsolicited struggle is inevitable.

So first and foremost accept the situation and analyze and understand why. Then start thinking and come up with solutions to make changes because you are never stuck. Execute your plans and watch them unfold.

I remember when I first moved out of my parents' house I had a pretty decent job. My hourly rate was probably four or five dollars higher than what the going rate was for people just striking out on their own typically back then. And from what I remember wages hadn't changed very much. Along the way I met people that made more money. But I also met quite a few people who made a whole lot less. I remember I had an apartment, car, insurance, home phone and light bill that were fixed bills every month meaning rain, sleet, or snow these were my monthly obligations. And on top of these bills were my food, gas, toiletries and entertainment.

Furnishing my new apartment looked like this. Cheap dishes, towels, bathroom decorations, pots and pans, one television and bed I brought from my bedroom at my parents' home, two new lawn chairs and my clothes. I was set. I was excited and life was good.

When my lease was up I moved because I figured out that my apartment wasn't the best or safest when my neighbor told me a guy beat his girlfriend up in the courtyard over the weekend and sent her to the emergency room and I saw dried blood on the sidewalk from someone being shot. I realized then that security and safety was something you pay for in an apartment by leasing something a little more expensive in a little bit nicer part of town.

As I made more money I bought nicer things and lived in nicer apartments and homes over time. My taste became fairly expensive and so did my budget. After I coupled together a few bad decisions and relationships along with a down economy I was swimming in debt. From credit cards, bank loans, mortgages and second car payments to extra miscellaneous stuff like vacationing and other luxuries. I found myself struggling financially and not being able to make ends meet.

Early on in life young people sometimes struggle financially because they usually have a hard time finding a job that pays fairly decent or they don't bother to find out who's paying more and just grab the first job that comes along. When you mix in a lack of planning and in most cases no budget or just spend. That's where the struggle begins. Living without financial perspective is usually the start.

Envision living on your own paying your bills by yourself. Just starting out at the age of eighteen or twenty realistically it's probably going to be tuff. Now, what if there's a kid involved. We won't talk about this just yet but think about it for a moment.

People struggle in life day in and day out young and old and the old usually have struggles their whole life. I've met people forty, fifty, and sixty years old who have never owned a car or a home and have never been on vacation.

They've spent their entire lives on some sort of government assistance and riding public transportation because that was their choice. No one has to be a product of the environment that they were raised in.

Struggling should force you to start working to change your situation really quick. Put a pencil to it and figure out if you need to have more discipline when it comes to spending; or if your ends just don't meet. In other words, you just don't make enough money to afford where you are in life. If that's the case start to trim the budget. And sometimes people barely make enough just to, "get by". Month in month out its tight and when the smallest issue comes up it's a life crisis. For example, some people are not able to pay the light bill because of needing a new car tire. Early in my life I met several people who lived like this. And even later in life, I've met several people who live like this. Either you choose to do or you choose not to do.

When money is tight and you're struggling always find a second job or start an at home business. There are a bunch of multilevel marketing opportunities out there that have really great potential if you make them work. A 15 thousand dollar part time job or opportunity added with a 25 or 30 thousand dollar full time job makes a really big difference in income and your level of comfort. Again, remember when I talked about being young with a child? I've met quite a few people that sell real estate part time. It eventually became full time and some of them got broker licenses and started their own agencies.

When it comes to life's ups and downs know that the decisions you make will in most cases directly affect when, where, how, why, and if you struggle financially.

What is all this talk about Credit?

When I graduated high school and went to college there were people at the doors to greet the students and welcome us all to the university. They had gifts for us. T-shirts, mugs, flashlights and all sorts of junk they were giving away. And all we had to do was sign. I'm telling you now please don't do it. Credit cards! I irresponsibly mismanaged my credit cards horribly, paid late and maxed them out. I was in college; but I was not educated when it came to credit and credit score management.

Interest! What's that? I was eaten alive and didn't know it. My parents never taught me about this stuff. But I learned the hard way.

From 2000 to 2006 I took a course on credit that cost me nearly twenty five thousand dollars. I was on my good job for about a year and was making pretty good money. Everyone on the job was either buying a new car or already had one and you know what, I was buying me one too. I gave the dealership five thousand dollars down plus a trade in and they gave me three thousand dollars credit for my trade. I was so excited to drive my new vehicle off the lot after waiting for nearly a month for them to decide to let me purchase it. They told me it took so long because they had to package my loan with 24 other loans to get mine to go through. I didn't care! The idea of that new car smell I could practically taste it. I was in love with my new SUV.

When I got to work a few days later one of my older coworkers asked me about my vehicle. He asked me about the interest rate, monthly payment and terms. I didn't mind talking because he was a nice guy and he told me about his auto transaction also. I couldn't really answer his questions because I didn't know. His monthly note was $30.00 higher than mine and his vehicle cost thirty five thousand dollars more than mine. He had zero percent interest (there go that strange word again) and I had high credit card interest compounded daily.

Years later, after I paid my vehicle off, I got into real estate and learned about credit, scores, and interest rates. More importantly I learned what to do to repair and maintain my credit. I found the old agreement on that SUV and saw that I paid more than twice for it due to interest.The trade in money was charged back to me on the back end and I gave my car away for free.

This was an expensive lesson to learn. I paid for it and I'm sharing this with you because I don't want you to buy this lesson. Learn it here for free.

Here are some simple rules to abide by in reference to your credit.

It's yours don't let anyone else use it. Buy nothing, lease nothing, rent nothing, co-sign nothing for anyone else. If they're asking it's because they have credit issues. If they didn't take care of theirs they won't think twice about ruining yours. No cell phones,no apartments. no apartments. They'll be gone you'll be paying the bill. Due dates, pay on or before the date due. This will build your credit. Watch out for late fees and absolutely do not pay late pass thirty days. It will report negatively and will lower your scores. Interest rates- the lower the better. Use 0%for the full term and transfer balances to 0%cards when you get one. Department store cards you do not need ever. They have the highest interest rates. Spend less - never max out your credit card. Pay it off every month. Never use more than one half the cards limit.

Usually creditors like to extend credit to people that show they can manage it.

Now, in reality just starting out you probably won't have the extra money needed to pay off your card every month. Notice credit card in the previous sentence is not plural. Which means you should only have one to two. You'll see people with five or ten don't do it they're too hard to manage because the interest will eat your little butte alive.

Penalties and interest are how the credit card companies and banking institutions get rich. Ten dollars here and Thirty five dollars there, it all adds up. These companies make billions because of young people starting out that don't know and old fools stuck in their ways that live in their ignorance too.

Here's an example for you.

It's your birthday and you take your credit card and spend $150.00 on an outfit for tonight. Your friends treat you; but you decide to buy a round of drinks at $100.00. When the statement comes it says balance due $250.00, minimum payment $25.00 and your interest rate is 11%. You need to pay it off in full. Because the interest is designed to never let you pay the card off. If you pay the minimum for 6 months the minimum due would go up every month and so would the balance due. In six months your balance due would more than double. Within a year you would owe well over a thousand dollars.

I remember when I was young and about your age I went through this myself and so did several of my friends. Mismanaging your credit is something you need to avoid doing. It will cost you double and triple in your life. You'll meet people driving new luxury cars, vacationing, buying homes, and getting jobs in careers you dreamed about while you sit on the sideline of life. You'll have to work harder and manage with less. I did it to myself and I don't want you to do it to yourself. Plus, let me reiterate, bad credit will cause the doors to certain careers to be locked when you go to open them for example, some government jobs and some private sector jobs worth having.

Cherish your credit. Love your credit because it's one of your best assets in life's "survival tool kit".

Communication is Key

In my life I've made plenty of mistakes and went without some things that I needed. Sometimes it was money, food, or just somebody to talk to and share my thoughts with. I realized later in life I didn't have to really do any of this. I've racked my brains in situations for months trying to figure things out. Tired, stressed and losing sleep when I just didn't know what to do. Then all of a sudden after talking with someone the problem was solved just like that. And it was over because I knew exactly what to do and how to handle it. I realized I let things be often harder than what they really had to be.

Sometimes in life, for whatever reason, we choose to keep things secret; or feel like we don't have anywhere to turn but that's never the case. Family, friends, coworkers, neighbors and church members are all available to lend an ear to listen and give support when needed. There are counselors and therapists who get paid to listen if you should ever find the need to seek professional help.

You are never alone. No matter where you are or what you're going through. It's ok to talk about it and share because chances are someone else can help base on a similar situation through firsthand experience or knows someone else who has been through that situation. Know that the key word is "through". Nothing is for always.

I remember in my life going on a few "first dates", with several very nice young ladies. I recall meeting them at a parents or a friends' house and even showing my driver license to show proof that I was actually who I said I was. I recall being walked to the car and even being snapped in a photograph with that person just in case. I thought it was funny at the time; but as I got to know them they explained later that's how they were being careful. As I got older and started watching the news, I saw how often innocent situations get blown out of proportion and people are victimized daily. I've even heard situations where the mothers were saying they never met the guy, didn't know his name, didn't know what he was driving, didn't have a phone number and the daughters cell phone was dead.

Always let someone know what's going on in your life. If you met somebody and everything started out great; but now he's abusive and you're afraid of him and scared to leave because of what you think he might do. I'm telling you not talking and getting help is the worst thing to do and the biggest mistake.

If you've gotten caught up in a situation where someone or a group of people are bullying or threatening to do bodily harm to you then please let someone know. People often come up missing, hurt or dead and nobody really knows what happened or who or how it started.

Meet a stranger in passing and now every time you look up he's there. At your apartment complex, near your car, at your job, or you realized he followed you home let someone know quickly. Call 911! Go stay a few days with a friend.

These are all signs of danger that can escalate without notice. Pay attention to your surroundings and to what's going on in your everyday life. Inform someone especially when something doesn't feel right. Trust your gut instinct.

I remember shortly after my mom passed away I moved back home with my dad for a while. I was grown and on my own. I was my own man. I remember my dad would call me at 1 or 2 o'clock in the morning wanting to know where I was and if I was ok. I couldn't stand it. I was grown. Get out of my business dad. That's how I felt. But later I realized I was wrong. After watching the news and seeing all the people my age coming up missing in the middle of the night. Being gunned down at the street light intersection for no apparent reason and robbed and killed at the gas station while coming home from a club. I realized my dad cared for my safety and about me. He wasn't being nosy. He was being concerned because he love me. And over the years I saw that it wasn't much he wouldn't do for me.

Now that I'm older I don't hesitate to tell him, one of my siblings or a friend where I'm going. Or better yet the who's, the what's, the when's, the where's, the how's and yep even sometimes the why's. And they all do the same.

I'm encouraging you to share the details of your life too because not only are they just as important; but because it's for your safety as well. And as you get older you will understand more and more but for now if you don't, just trust me.

Eating Healthy
Diet and Exercise

My daughter by no means am I an expert on this subject. I'm not claiming to have everything under control either. But I need you to know that it's important to eat healthy, diet and exercise. These things are essential for a long good quality life. When I was young these things didn't matter because I did not know and they did not affect me. Later in life I started hearing words like cholesterol, carbohydrates, high blood pressure, diabetes and so on and so forth. As I got older these words became more important to me because I saw that along with these words come medications and I see this first hand on a weekly basis in my current career. Illnesses are very serious and due to poor health, obesity, and a lack of awareness and in most cases and can eventually cause death if left untreated.

As my eyes became open to the situation I started to notice that older people in my neighborhood were walking in the mornings and evenings. I began to witness there were very few older people eating at the fast food restaurants. And when they were there they would order things like grilled, diet and no cheese. As I started doing my research I eventually began to cut back on foods like pizza, and hamburgers, and all types of greasy foods and began eating more foods that were fresh, raw, organic, vegetables, and salmon. I got away from eating mostly red meats to chicken, turkey and fish. Instead of drinking sugars like sodas and juices I started drinking mostly water.

Over the years I recognized my clothes got tighter, I went a few sizes bigger and so did my belt and my belly. My energy level went out the door. I was tired all the time and slept all the time. My daughter It's important to pay attention to the signs as your body changes because it's good to get on top of weight gain right away and not let it go on for years.

I'm telling you this why you're still young so if the time should ever come you can make adjustments quickly. Certain foods you'll leave alone all together and others you'll probably need to just cut back. Remember everything in moderation.

Incorporate exercise into your routine as often as possible and eventually make it apart of your everyday life. Now days I try to watch what I eat, drink fresh juice, take the stairs at work, go to the gym and ride my bicycle. I also found a good vitamin to be very essential and a step in the right direction to help add the missing nutrients much needed. Food isn't as nutritional as it used to be. And periodically you need to detox and cleanse your body. When it comes to diet I'm not talking about all the gimmicks you hear about. I'm simply talking about the food choices you make daily. In my twenties I chose to eat mostly fast foods; but as I've gotten older I realized raw fruits and vegetables is the way to go as much as possible.

I believe I'm moving in the right direction but I would be better off if I would have paid closer attention earlier in life. Do your own research to figure out what foods to eat and which ones to skip as you get older. And always remember, as my uncle would say to me, "An ounce of prevention is worth more than a pound of cure". It all starts with what we eat.

Learn to eat healthy my daughter, detox your body periodically and exercise. It will make a world of difference.

Relationships and Marriage

My daughter, know that when it comes to relationships the idea of a relationship is always nice and very beautiful. But know upfront sometimes they work and sometimes they don't. It depends on how it's set up from the very beginning. If it's not correct from the start chances are it's probably not going to work.

Relationships are win-win young lady. And everybody has an angle. You hear men say all the time, "She's pretty, I like her personality, we clicked and she was it". They don't tell you it helped that she was a supervisor or a school teacher and made pretty good money. He was tall and handsome with a great physique; but we didn't work out. Why? Because he was sneaky and I couldn't trust him. Something just didn't seem right with him, (Down Low).

Make no mistake my daughter women marry drunks and womanizers all the time and men marry women with issues too. But they go into the relationship with their eyes wide open based on their needs and wants.

Women say, He's a drunk; but he got a great career, pays the bills and I get to stay at home. He travel nonstop with his job; but we're financially secure. Or, she can't keep a job;

but I had to have her. That's one thing you hear men say.

My daughter the list goes on and on. Understand in order for the relationship to work everybody has to get part of what they want if they are lucky coupled with all of what they need. Always know upfront, if he's not getting out of the deal what he wants and needs chances are he's not happy and not going to stay. He may be there temporarily; but long term he won't stay. This is why people date for three or four years and move on. Or divorce after a year or two. So, you see, if the relationship is not working for the both of you it's not going to last. This is also the main reason why people cheat.

My daughter when it comes to relationships a solid foundation is the key.

I believe a solid foundation has the ingredients to build everlasting bonds. Strong bonds will withstand the test of time, imperfections, shortcomings, mistakes and sometimes weaknesses. The foundation should be made up of open communication, trust, honesty and forgiveness coupled with patience and kindness. With this, there is everlasting love, respect and friendship.

Remember, always be true and honest to the most important person in your life from the beginning and that's you. Always think "me first", especially when it's just you because you better believe he is. Learn to think with your head and not with your heart from the beginning.

For example, over the course of a few months you meet ten guys because of the places you go and people you know. All these guys are interested in you. Seven guys work and three don't. Out of the seven, three kind of rub you the wrong way right from the start; but one of the three is very cute with gorgeous eyes, a great smile and a superhot body. So you decided to date him first. Only to find out he's aggressive and verbally abusive. The date went horribly wrong and he was ready to beat you like a piñata. So now you have how many guys left to choose from?

Women usually never make it to the last few guys. They usually pick wrong in the first round and try to stick it out with him. That's why you see so many women who are unhappily chained in dead end relationships. They work, have children and make the most of it ; but ultimately they are unhappy. And after looking at the example you probably stand a better chance dating one of the remaining four; or all four to figure out which one you like best.

Always know the dynamics and functions of the relationship you are about to enter. For example, shorts are never acceptable as trousers and no one says let me grab my coat while reaching for a T-shirt. In other words, some people you date. Some people you marry. Some people, you play with, and others you.... well, just ignore altogether. And people you get involved with view you the same way. So be cautious.

When you finally decide you're ready for a long term commitment that eventually leads to marriage hopefully he'll come along and find you. Don't go looking for him. **Position yourself to be found. Be somebody worth finding. Become a "Good Thing".**

And When you meet that right guy he will want to help you meet your needs and wants and will be in a position to help or seriously working on getting there. He'll actually want to take care of you mentally, emotionally and physically. Even though you might make more money. He's not interested in drastically making withdrawals out of you and your life without any deposits. He's committed, and the idea of thinking long term may make him a bit nervous; and that's normal. After all it's a big step. But he's ready and willing to invest in a life with you.

And by the way, I believe in a man and a woman relationship. Not relationships between two men or two women. They happen, and they last; but this is not what was meant. Let's throw it all in the mix. I'm not intentionally trying to offend anyone. A relationship is a relationship and I don't have the final say so.

Know that when it comes to marriage I've got very limited experience; but I did figure out a few things. You better make sure you love him. You better make sure there's respect. You better make sure it's what you want because every marriage experience ups and downs, good times and bad. And when it gets rough you need to be prepared to fight for you marriage. And if the foundation is not right you won't have it in you to fight because it won't be worth it to you.

That's why so many marriages fall apart, people surrender and walk away.

A note from the Author

While writing this book my heart and my eyes were opened and I was allowed to see how there are so many young ladies in the world struggling day in and day out. Lacking hope and really not knowing where to go or turn. And that it's a never ending cycle.

We have to start reaching for our daughters, their friends, and classmates in the schools as early as eighth and ninth grade and cultivate them throughout high school getting them prepared for the things to come.

I am not perfect nor have I claimed to be; but I love my daughters as most men should. I refuse to stand by idly and watch the world take advantage of them and chew them up and spit them back out in pieces.